Let's Discover
BIRDS IN OUR WORLD

By Ada and Frank Graham, Jr.

Photography by Elaine Wickens

GOLDEN PRESS • NEW YORK

Western Publishing Company, Inc.
Racine, Wisconsin

This book is one of a series of Audubon Primers, sponsored by the National Audubon Society. Like the other books in the series, it is designed to focus on one particular aspect of the natural world. With you as a guide, a child's natural curiosity may be nurtured, directed and expanded.

This is a real story about real people. The adventures of the children and the discoveries they make are available to everyone. Read the story to children too young to read or make it available to those who can. It may prompt you and your young companion(s) to explore the world of nature. Exploring leads to discovery.

To prepare yourself for additional questions that may arise, refer to the "Key" on pages 44-45. It provides information that goes beyond the story itself. Besides being a useful reference, it may reawaken your own curiosity about the world in which you live.

The Authors:
Ada and Frank Graham, Jr.

Mankind has admired the beauty of birds' plumage and song for thousands of years, and has given them prominent roles in our art, literature and folklore. Many of us have envied their gift of flight.

At the same time, people have slaughtered them unmercifully for sport, for food and for decorating clothing with their beautiful plumage. We have exterminated them for encroaching on the plant and animal food supply we consider our very own.

To help preserve our remaining bird life, Audubon Societies were created at the end of the nineteenth century. To achieve their goal of promoting the conservation of wildlife and the natural environment, and the educating of man regarding his relationships with, and his place within the national environment as an ecological system, the National Audubon Society and its predecessors:

- Campaigned for strong laws to protect birds

- Devised education programs to help children and adults understand the marvelously varied world of birds and their role in helping to maintain an ecological balance

- Set aside sanctuaries where birds were able to feed, rest, and nest undisturbed by man.

- Conduct workshops which help to better equip teachers, youth leaders and other adults to import an understanding of man's role in nature, and the importance of conservation in our world today.

Watching birds, studying their behavior, and detecting their differences can be a gratifying pastime for both children and adults, as over twenty million bird watchers across the land can attest. This book attempts to introduce children to one facet of their natural world that may provide a lifetime of enjoyment.

This story is a real life adventure. It is the story of Philip and his growing awareness of the birds in his world. It involves discovery, as well as adventure.

Share this adventure with a young companion. But don't be surprised if you become eager to know more.

Invitation to Adventure

A fat little bird with an orange breast ran across the lawn. Philip watched it through the window.

"Look, Mom, a bird!" he called.

Philip's mother ran to the window. "That's a robin," she said. "It's probably looking for something to eat."

"He has something in his mouth already," said Philip. "It looks like a worm."

As Philip and his mother watched, the robin flew to a nearby tree and ate the rest of his worm. Then he dropped to the lawn again. He stood very still, turning his head from side to side, as if he were looking for something.

Suddenly, he snatched something from the ground with his pointed bill.

"He's got another worm!" Philip cried.

One end of the worm was in the robin's mouth and the other end was still in the ground. The robin tugged and tugged. The worm stretched and stretched. It seemed as if the worm would break in half. But, then the worm popped out of the ground, and the robin gobbled him up.

"Robins eat worms just like chickens do," said Philip.

His mother nodded, and said, "Look, the robin is flying away."

"Where is the robin going?" asked Philip.

"Perhaps there is a nest nearby, where the female lays its eggs," his mother said.

"Just like chickens?" asked Philip.

"Just like chickens," replied his mother. "All female birds lay eggs."

"Are chickens birds?" asked Philip.

"Yes," replied his mother.

Philip and his mother went out to the chicken coop in their backyard. They took some food for the chickens. There were many hens, but only two or three roosters.

Philip picked up two eggs from the nest. "Do only birds lay eggs?" asked Philip.

"No," said his mother. "Other kinds of animals lay eggs. Fishes and frogs and insects lay eggs too. But only the females lay eggs."

Philip ran after a chicken, but the chicken ran away from him, flapping its stubby little wings. A chicken's wings don't help very much. Chickens can only fly short distances and not very high.

"Other animals may have wings, but do you know something that birds have that no other animals have?" asked Philip's mother.

Philip wrinkled his forehead and wondered what was so special about a bird.

"Look down there!" said his mother as she pointed to the ground. Philip bent down and picked up something from the floor of the chicken coop.

"A feather?" he asked, and held it up to the light.

"Yes, a feather," said his mother. "Birds are the only animals that have feathers."

From that day on, Philip and his parents watched for birds wherever they went. They explored the wooded places near their house. They looked for birds among the trees where they perched and fed.

Sometimes the birds looked back at them.

Sometimes it was hard to see the tiny warblers. But, if Philip stood very still, and listened, he was sure to see one through the green leaves.

Philip and his father watched as a flock of birds flew overhead. They were flying north to their nesting grounds. There they would build nests and raise their young during the warm summer months.

One day, when Philip and his father went exploring, they discovered a nest with three eggs in it. Soon, baby birds would hatch from the eggs. Philip and his father were very careful not to disturb the nest.

In the evenings, Philip and his father would look at books about birds. Philip learned the names of many birds and what to look for when he saw them outdoors. He listened to records of their songs and soon he could recognize many of them by sound.

Philip looked for birds everywhere.

Another day, Philip and his mother went to the city. The sidewalks were noisy and crowded. Cars and trucks roared past them. The city was very different from the place where they lived.

As they crossed the street, a bird hopped in front of them. It was a little brown bird, and it had a twig in its bill.

"That's an English sparrow," said Philip's mother.

Philip watched the sparrow as it flew up and over the noisy traffic, and perched on a lamppost. There was a hole at the end of the metal bar. The sparrow disappeared into the hole.

"Look Philip, that sparrow must be building a nest inside that hole. It has a twig in its bill."

They watched for a few minutes before crossing the street.

Philip and his mother were on their way
to visit his friend, Trish. Trish and her
parents lived in an apartment in the city.
When they arrived at the apartment, Philip
told Trish about the sparrow building its
nest in the lamppost.

"Oh, we have many birds in the city,
too." Trish told Philip. "I see them from
my window every day."

Philip looked out the window. In the courtyard below was a small group of trees.

"See, there's a bird," said Trish. She pointed to a tree right below the window.

Later in the day, Trish went for a walk with Philip and his mother. They walked a short distance to the river. Gulls were flying over the oily-looking water. Some of them landed in a vacant lot nearby.

The gulls were large gray-and-white birds. Some of them had black heads. Their loud cries rang out as they soared in search of food.

"They sound funny," said Philip.

"The ones with the black heads are called 'laughing gulls'," Trish told him. "Listen! They sound as if they are laughing at something."

Philip liked to watch the gulls in flight. He liked to watch them take off and land.

Gulls, like most birds, are well made for flying. They have hollow bones, and strong wing muscles. Other muscles move their tail feathers and help them to steer.

Their wings are long and pointed and their tails are usually square.

Trish and Philip, and Philip's mother stopped in a nearby park.

There were many pigeons in the park. They were quite tame. They walked right up to Philip and took some popcorn he threw to them.

"Look," said Philip. "They have red toes." "And they only have four of them," said Trish. One of the pigeons walked so close to Philip that he could see that it had three toes in front and one behind.

"Most birds have four toes," said Philip's mother. "And see how they walk, with one foot in front of the other. Pigeons walk, sparrows hop, and robins run," she said.

Soon it was time to go home. As they left the park, they passed a tall building. Philip heard a noise and looked up. It was a soft noise and it sounded like $\overline{oo}$-$r\overline{oo}$-$c\overline{oo}$. Suddenly, he saw a pigeon through the bars covering the window.

"Look!" said Philip. "The pigeon has a nest on the window ledge."

"Yes," said Trish. "They don't mind people, and many people feed the pigeons every day. Pigeons build their nests on city buildings."

Philip was discovering that birds lived every-where in the city, too.

Photo by: Edward Schell

Photo by: Edward Schell

In the summertime, Philip noticed that the birds did not feed on the seeds he put out for them. He soon discovered it was because there were plenty of seeds and insects in the woods nearby.

But swallows were always near the house, chasing insects around the lawn. They built their nests in the birdhouses that Philip's father had made for them.

And redwing blackbirds were frequent visitors.

A cardinal nested in a bush near Philip's house. Its bright feathers were easy to see, and Philip soon learned that the male had brighter feathers than the female. It also had a thick bill that was good for crushing the hard shells of seeds.

Other birds, in the woods near his house, were busy taking care of their young. Their eggs had hatched and the young birds were always hungry.

Philip watched the parents fly back and forth to their nest, taking food to the young that waited with their mouths always open. The soft down that covered their bodies, would soon be replaced with feathers.

Photo by: Edward Schell

© National Audubon Society

Philip listened to the sounds in the woods. He heard the woodpecker's *tap-tap-tap,* as it pecked at the holes in the tree trunk. Its strong, sharp bill, hammered to make the hole large enough to reach the insect larva that was hiding inside.

Philip heard an owl hoot in the distance. He quietly walked toward the sound, and spied the owl perched in a tree. Owls hunt at night and are not easy to find in the daytime.

Photo by: Edward Schell

Soon, the summer came to an end. Autumn had come, and Philip and his mother took walks down to the pond. They liked to watch the ducks and swans swim and feed.

The ducks paddled through the water with their webbed feet. They poked their heads beneath the water to scoop up pond weeds with their broad flat bills. The autumn sun made their feathers shine.

"Don't they get cold?" asked Philip.

"No," said his mother. "Their feathers keep them warm and dry."

It was fun to watch them nudge one another.

There were other birds at the pond too. Philip watched two grackles walking near the shore. They were looking for seeds and insects. Their shiny black feathers kept them warm and dry. Philip noticed they did not have webbed feet, as ducks and other waterfowl do. They just waded near the edges.

It would soon be winter. The seeds and insects would be scarce and the birds would have to look harder for their food.

That day, when Philip and his mother got home from the pond, they hung a bird feeder in a tree. They filled it with seeds so the birds would be sure to come all winter long.

"Some birds will fly south for the winter," said Philip's mother. "Tomorrow, we will go to the bird sanctuary, and watch the birds that stop there to rest and feed. Trish can go with us," she said.

The next day, Philip and his parents took
Trish to the bird sanctuary.

The sanctuary had water all around it, and
lots of tall grasses which help to protect
the many birds there.

Philip and Trish ran toward a pond.
Suddenly, two ducks flew up as Trish came
near. Philip's father took a picture of them
just as they flew over some low pine trees.
They all watched as the ducks quickly turned,
and gracefully landed on the pond again.

Trish discovered a nest in some low bushes and called to Philip to come and see. It was a small nest. And now it was empty.

But there were many birds all around them in the sanctuary. Two Canada Geese swam by in the water and some gulls were flying overhead.

"May I see through the binoculars?" asked Trish. Philip's father handed them to her. Trish looked first at the gulls, then at the geese. The binoculars made the geese seem very close.

Photo by: Edward Schell

Photo by: Edward Schell

A long-legged egret waded through the water. It stopped and stood very still, as if it were watching something. Suddenly, it stretched its long neck into the water and grabbed a fish in its sharp bill.

Sandpipers walked along the shore, looking for tiny sea creatures.

Photo by: Les Line

A smaller shorebird, the plover, stayed on the drier parts of the shore looking for food.

Philip ran over to Trish and said, "I want to see too." And Trish handed him the binoculars.

"I don't see anything," said Philip. And everybody laughed.

"That's because you have your fingers over the lens," his father said. "Hold them the way Trish did."

"Now I can see," said Philip. He laughed, too.

Three terns stood near each other on the sand. They were busy turning their heads this way and that. They ruffled their feathers with their black and red bills.

"Those terns are preening," said Philip's mother. "They are cleaning and setting their feathers, getting them ready for the long flight south."

Suddenly the terns stopped preening.
They shook themselves all over, letting
their feathers fall into place. They flew a
short distance, stopped briefly on some
rocks, and then took off. Their long wings
flapped gracefully, as they headed south
where they would spend the winter.

"Look at their tails," said Philip's father.
"They have forked tails."

By now, Philip had
seen birds in many
places. He had seen
sparrows, gulls, and
pigeons in the city.
He had seen ducks and
grackles at the pond.
He had seen egrets and
sandpipers, and geese,
terns and plovers in
the sanctuary. He had
learned to call them by
name. He had discovered
a world of birds.

But Philip discovered
that his favorite birds
were the ones that
flocked right around his
own house. To Philip
and his parents these
birds were their friends.

A Key to Discovery

Take your first step into the world of birds, by bringing with you some basic information and a few facts. If you do, you will help to quicken your curiosity about the colorful and lively life of birds.

Birds are everywhere. No single place is best for observing them, from a salt water marsh; to shore areas; to a wooded park in the midst of a city. But first, explore your own locality. You will discover certain spots are favored by certain birds.

Early morning is the best time of day for bird-watching. The essential equipment: a pair of good eyes and good ears. Both of these senses are keen in young children.

Walk slowly and quietly. Conceal yourself if possible. Do not wear bright clothing. Field glasses or binoculars are of great value in bringing tree-top birds down to you. Sit quietly in a likely spot and let the birds come to you.

Make bird-watching a year-round activity. Each season offers surprises and delights to careful observers.

As you observe, you will detect differences among birds: the shape of their bills; the shape and size of their legs; prominent markings on their head, wings or tails. Here are some facts you may begin to observe on your first adventure into the world of birds.

BILLS

Cardinals, sparrows and *finches* have short conical bills for cracking the hard casing of seeds.

Warblers and *chickadees* have thin bills that are good for picking insects off leaves or barks.

Ducks have broad flat bills for scooping seeds or tiny organisms out of the mud and water.

SIZE AND SHAPE

Swallows and *hummingbirds* have small legs and feet. They get most of their food while flying, and have little need for walking.

Herons and *flamingos* have long legs. They find their food by wading through the water near the shore.

Hawks have long sharp claws for grasping their prey.

FEATHERS

Feathers make birds distinct from all other living things. Some kinds of birds are practically naked when they hatch. But soon, a soft down covers their bodies. As they grow, so do their feathers. Feathers carry the specific markings that distinguish one kind of bird from another. Sometimes feathers are clues to the bird's name. For example: bluebirds, red-winged blackbirds, scarlet tanagers and red-tailed hawks.

VOICES

If you listen carefully, you will begin to be able to identify birds by their voices. These voices have a function. For instance, birds use song to warn other birds of their own kind away from their breeding territory. So listen for their sounds. Ducks *quack*, owls *hoot*, crows *caw*, doves *coo*, and song birds *sing*. So, do much of your watching with your ears, and you too may become an expert.

MIGRATION

Notice that the bird life around your home changes with the seasons. Migrating birds spend the winter in sunny climates, and then in the spring, fly north to build nests and raise their young. Their powerful wing muscles, their hollow bones, and their weightless covering of feathers help make birds efficient flying machines.

However, some birds are residential all year. *Crows, chickadees* and *house sparrows* for instance, may remain near their breeding ground all winter, or move only short distances in search of food.

FAMILIES

Families of birds are made up of a number of related species. There are many different kinds of *ducks, owls,* and *sparrows.* For example there are *mallard ducks, black ducks, wood ducks.* There are about 750 different kinds of birds which live, or occasionally visit, the United States and Canada. The pictures in this book will help you recognize some characteristics of some bird families. Another valuable tool is a set of bird cards, available through an Audubon Society or a local nature center. Through these large clear pictures, you will soon become familiar with the habits and markings of a great variety of birds.

As your interest grows and if you wish to extend your knowledge about *Birds In Our World,* obtain some of the excellent books available on the subject. (See *For Further Reading,* on this page.)

After reading this book to your child or a young companion(s), set out on an adventure together. You will discover that learning about birds is really learning about life. You can follow with increasing understanding the life cycle of birds, from courtship and nest building; to the development of a family of birds; to the parents tending their young. This discovery can become an important part of a young child's learning experience. In such an experience may lie the roots of an enduring reverence for all life.

FOR FURTHER READING

Austin, Oliver, L., Jr., Birds of the World, *Golden Press, New York, 1961.*

Peterson, Roger T., A Field Guide to the Birds, (eastern land and water birds), *Houghton Mifflin Co., Boston, 1947;* A Field Guide to Western Birds, *Houghton Mifflin Co., Boston, 1961.*

Robbins, Chandler S., Bruun, Bertel, and Zim, Herbert S., Birds of North America, A Guide to Field Identification, *Golden Press, New York, 1966.*

Zim, Herbert S., and Gabrielson, Ira N., Birds, A Guide to the Most Familiar American Birds, *Golden Press, New York, 1956.*

Audubon, published by the National Audubon Society, 950 Third Avenue, New York.